Science at the Edge

Forensic Science

Ann Fullick

Heinemann
LIBRARY
Chicago, Illinois

© 2006 Heinemann Library
a division of Reed Elsevier Inc.
Chicago, Illinois

Customer Service 888-454-2279

Visit our website at www.heinemannlibrary.com

Illustrations by Jeff Edwards
Originated by Repro Multi Warna
Printed and bound in China by SCPC Company Limited

10 09 08 07 06
10 9 8 7 6 5 4 3 2 1

Library of Congress Cataloging-in-Publication Data
Fullick, Ann, 1956-
  Forensic science / Ann Fullick.
    p. cm. -- (Science at the edge)
  Includes index.
  ISBN 1-4034-7763-9 (library binding - hardcover)
  1. Forensic sciences--Juvenile literature. 2. Criminal investigation--Juvenile literature. I. Title. II. Series.
  HV8073.F775 2005
  363.25--dc22

                          2005024170

Acknowledgements
The Publishers would like to thank the following for permission to reproduce photographs: Alamy Images/Jack Sullivan p**20**, Ardea (P Morris) p**16**; Associated Press (South Tyrol Museum of Archaeology) p**15**; Corbis/Ed Kashi p**54**; Corbis (Marco Cauz) p**5**; Corbis/Peter Yates p**52**; Corbis Sygma (Greg English) p**48**, (Corbis/ Bettman) p**39**; Harcourt Education Ltd p**29**; Getty Images/Robert Harding p**30**; Kelly Duckett p**7**; Reuters/HO p**33** left & right; Rex Features pp**23**, **42**, (Andrew Drysdale/ADR) p**51**, (Avantis/Ixo) p**30**, (Jim Pickerell) p**34**, (Sipa Press) p**36**; Science Photo Library p**57**, (Alfred Pasieka) p**24**, (Cetus Corporation, Peter Arnold Inc) p**49**, (Costantino Margiotta) p**12**, (Eye of Science) p**25**, (Mauro Fermariello) p**45**, (Neville Chadwick) p**47**, (Pascal Goetgheluck) p**6**, (Philippe Plailly) p**10**, (Prof K Seddon & Dr T Evans, Queen's University Belfast) p**44**; Topham (AP) p**31**, (David Frazier/The Image Works) p**40**, (Photonews Service/Old Bailey) p**11**, (PressNet) p**4**, (The Image Works) p**53**, (The Image Works/Joe Sohm) p**27**, (The Image Works/Kent Meireis) p**28**

Cover photograph of a forensic blood sample reproduced with permission of Science Photo Library (Dr Jurgen Scriba).

The Publishers would like to thank Dr. Allen Anscombe, Forensic Pathologist, for his assistance in the preparation of this book.

Every effort has been made to contact copyright holders of any material reproduced in this book. Any omissions will be rectified in subsequent printings if notice is given to the Publishers.

Disclaimer
All the Internet addresses (URLs) given in this book were valid at the time of going to press. However, due to the dynamic nature of the Internet, some addresses may have changed, or sites may have changed or ceased to exist since publication. While the author and the Publishers regret any inconvenience this may cause readers, no responsibility for any such changes can be accepted by either the author or the Publishers.

Contents

Helena's Story

Forensic science is the science of the investigation of crime. It involves an amazing number of different techniques, some of which are still controversial. However, the story of Helena Greenwood clearly shows the important role of modern forensic science in bringing criminals to justice.

Helena Greenwood was a talented British biochemist. In 1977 she moved to the United States with her husband Roger Franklin, settling in a town where Helena worked as a researcher specializing in DNA. In 1984, a burglar, David Frediani, broke into their house while Helena was at home. Frediani held Helena at gunpoint for several hours and assaulted her. She managed to persuade him not to kill her by saying that she would never contact the police. Of course, after he left, she called the police immediately, and from her description they found Frediani. He was granted bail and a trial date was set for 1985. Helena and Roger were afraid that Frediani might attack again, so when Helena was offered a job in San Diego that continued her work on DNA, they were pleased to move. But in August 1985, things went terribly wrong.

Helena Greenwood had no idea that her work on DNA analysis, which she loved, would one day help track down her brutal attacker.

A second attack

Three weeks before David Frediani was due to go on trial for burglary and assault, Roger found Helena dead in their yard. She had been strangled and beaten. Frediani was the main suspect, but although police found evidence from his credit cards that he had been in the area just before the murder, they had no forensic evidence linking him to Helena's body. Frediani stood trial for the original assault and went to prison for six years, although he was released after only three. No one could find any proof that he was involved in Helena's violent death, but no other suspects emerged.

Then, in 1999, the San Diego police decided to reopen a number of unsolved murders to see if new forensic techniques based on DNA fingerprinting could help them.

Skin fragments had been found under Helena's fingernails when her body was examined. It was skin from her attacker, which she had scratched off when she struggled with him. The DNA from this skin was analyzed and was found to match that of David Frediani. For many years he had lived an apparently normal life, probably thinking he had gotten away with his terrible crime. But the development of modern forensic techniques, based partly on the work of the woman he killed, eventually led to his capture and conviction. More than 15 years after he killed Helena Greenwood, Frediani was tried, found guilty, and sentenced to life imprisonment.

Modern forensic science can use tiny scraps of evidence, like substances trapped behind the fingernails of a victim, to prove the guilt or innocence of a suspect.

The Fight for Justice

In every country of the world, crimes are committed. Police forces around the world are constantly working to catch and convict criminals who break the law.

In many countries, it is not enough for the police to accuse someone of committing a crime. The justice system demands evidence that proves beyond all reasonable doubt that a particular person has committed a particular crime. This is where forensic science comes in.

Every contact leaves a trace

Wherever you go, whatever you do, you leave behind traces of your activity. These might be fingerprints or footprints, threads from your clothing, flakes of skin, or perhaps even an ear print! Even the most careful criminal will leave behind traces after a crime, and these are what the police and forensic scientists aim to find and identify. When a crime has been committed or an accident has happened, the scene will contain many of these tiny clues to how it happened. These form an important part of

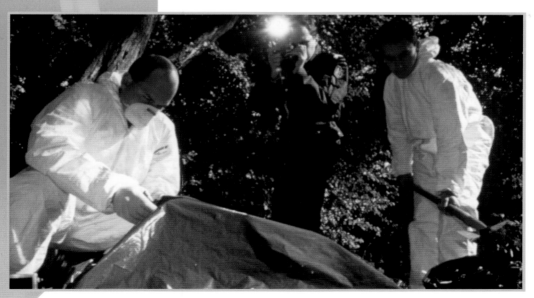

When a serious crime has been committed, specially trained police officers known as crime scene investigators, or CSI, seal off the area to collect evidence for forensic examination.

what the police have to work on in order to identify a criminal or to understand the cause of an accident. Then forensic scientists examine the clues using forensic technology to try to solve the crime. Forensic science should be able to prove with 100 percent certainty that a particular individual committed a crime. Perhaps even more importantly, it should be able to show that a wrongly accused individual is innocent.

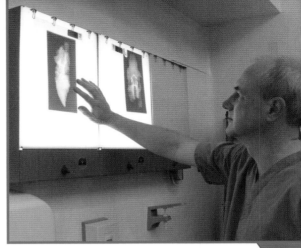

Dr. Allen Anscombe is a forensic pathologist (doctor that studies disease). He says his work is interesting because he never sees the same thing twice.

The answer to everything?

The forensic techniques you will read about in this book set out to make it ever more likely that someone who commits a crime, however small, will be identified and brought to justice. The aim is to get more convictions and reduce crime by developing better methods of reliably identifying criminals.

Unfortunately, things do not always work out quite so well in practice. It is true that as forensic science has developed, it has become increasingly possible to solve crimes effectively. But this does not stop people from committing crimes, although it does increase the likelihood that they will be caught. All too often, lack of resources means that forensic examinations are limited to bigger crimes. Investigations into the sort of crime that affects most people—small theft, muggings, and burglaries—often do not benefit from the latest developments in forensic techniques.

One of the most serious situations that can arise in the investigation of a crime is when an innocent person is accused and convicted of a crime he or she did not commit. Developments in forensic science—such as DNA technology, spectrometers, and sophisticated computer programs that analyze fingerprints—are helping to make sure that wrongful convictions happen less and less. But human error, biased opinions, and corruption can still give rise to wrongful convictions, and technology is not always perfect. Still, the goal of forensic science is to uncover the truth behind every crime.

Fingerprints

The scene of a crime has to be processed. This means it is sealed off and photographed, and anything that might yield a clue to the identity of the criminal is collected and labeled. This evidence must be closely watched at all times, from its collection at the scene of a crime to its appearance in a court of law, to make sure no one has tampered with or damaged it. One of the best-known forms of evidence that can tie a particular person to the scene of a crime is a fingerprint.

What are fingerprints?

Fingerprints are the patterns of ridges in the skin of the fingertips. They are formed before you are born, as you develop in your mother's womb, and they never change during your lifetime unless the ends of your fingers are severely damaged. They form one of three basic patterns: swirls, loops, and arches. Within each of these basic patterns there are small variations, known as minutiae points, and it is these tiny difference points that make our fingerprints unique. No two people have the same arrangement of minutiae points in their fingerprints, even if the basic patterns are similar.

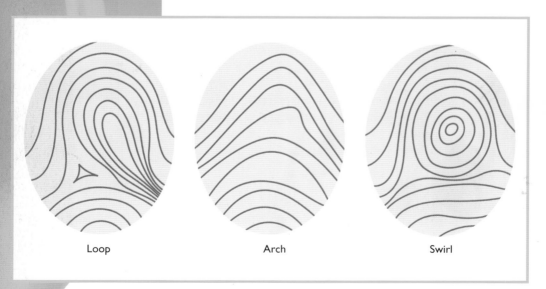

Loop   Arch   Swirl

This shows the three basic fingertip patterns. Even identical twins don't have identical fingerprints. It has been calculated that the chance of two people having the same pattern is one in 64 billion!

Chinese fingerprint folklore

Ancient Chinese folklore says that certain fingerprint patterns are linked to different destinies. Here are a selection of them:

- one swirl indicates poverty
- two swirls indicate riches
- three and four swirls mean you will open a pawnshop
- five swirls for a mediator (someone who helps two parties communicate)
- six swirls for a thief
- seven swirls means many problems in your life
- eight swirls and you will eat chaff (the waste part of the grain)
- nine swirls with a loop mean you will be rich, doing no work but eating well until your old age.

You leave fingerprints on many of the different surfaces you touch as you go through life. The patterns are left behind in traces of sweat and oil from your skin.

Classification

In 1892 Sir Francis Galton (Charles Darwin's cousin) published a book that included the first classification system for fingerprints. Galton actually took many of his ideas from the work of Henry Faulds. Faulds figured out the importance of fingerprints, but because he was poor and had a low position in society, he was ignored. So he wrote to Galton asking for help, and Galton used the material himself!

The first recorded use of fingerprints to catch a criminal was by the Argentinean police officer Juan Vucetich in 1892. A woman claimed that someone had murdered her two sons and attempted to murder her. But Vucetich found her bloody fingerprint at the crime scene, and this proved that she had murdered her own sons.

Since then fingerprints have become a very important tool for the forensic investigator, used around the world to convict criminals. But collecting and identifying fingerprints is not easy, and increasingly complex methods are used to make sure this form of evidence remains a useful tool.

Collecting fingerprints

The traditional method for collecting fingerprints from flat surfaces like glass is powder processing. In this method, the area is brushed with powder, and tiny particles stick to the lines of the fingerprint. The print is then lifted using tape, transferred to paper, and photographed so that the details can be magnified easily for detailed identification. One modern process involves exposing fingerprints to iodine fumes, which turn them purple. Another involves using superglue, which clumps and sticks inside the details of the fingerprint, setting in seconds, and giving clear details of the print on a wider variety of materials than glass.

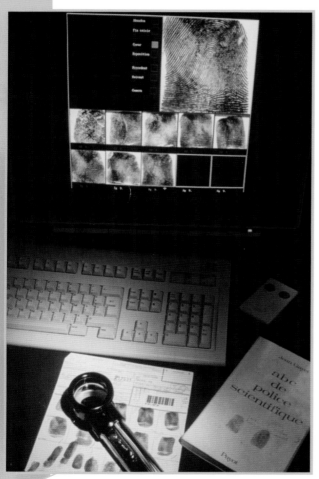

Special lighting techniques and fluorescent dyes have made it possible to collect fingerprints from almost any surface. It is even possible to take fingerprints from objects that have been underwater.

For many years, identifying fingerprints was a difficult task, which involved comparing the prints from a crime scene with those of known criminals, suspects, and innocent people from the area. Now, with computers, it is much easier. Fingerprints from known criminals all over the United States are stored in a computer database called IAFIS (Integrated Automated Fingerprint Identification System). Police officers from all over the country can access the database from anywhere and have results within two hours!

IAFIS contains the fingerprints of more then 47 million subjects! Hundreds and thousands of criminals have been identified using the new technology, many of whom might have escaped identification in the past.

Are prints always right?

The short answer is yes, but it is not that simple. As criminals have become increasingly aware of the use of fingerprints to convict them, they have been more careful not to leave them at crime scenes. Wearing gloves, for example, greatly reduces the chance of leaving useful prints. Also, fingerprints can be moved. For instance, a fingerprint left on a glass in one place could be transferred to another place entirely, using nothing more complicated than a piece of transparent tape. This raised the possibility of people being set up by other criminals or crooked elements in the police force. For a while it even made people doubt the reliability of fingerprint evidence.

Footprints and ear prints

Fingerprints are not the only evidence that criminals leave behind. Footprints can be photographed using special lighting to show the details of the imprint, and casts can be made for direct comparison with shoes found later. Although lots of people wear the same type of shoe, everyone walks in a different way, so shoe prints are often unique to the individual shoe.

Perhaps weirdest of all, criminals have been known to leave ear prints at crime scenes. These have been used to identify and convict people! However, a man convicted on ear-print evidence alone was freed on appeal in 2004, and doubts about the safety of this method are growing.

Some experts think that ear prints are as unique to the individual as fingerprints, and they have been used to prove that an individual was at the scene of a crime.

Blood and Body Parts

When a murder is committed, it is extremely important to get as much evidence as possible from the body. When anyone dies unexpectedly, a specially trained doctor called a pathologist will examine him or her. They will carry out an operation known as an autopsy on the dead body. The purpose of the autopsy is to find out about the person's health before death and to learn how she or he died. If there is any suspicion of murder, then the autopsy will be carried out by a forensic pathologist—a pathologist who is a specialist in changes in the body that might be due to criminal activity.

Autopsy means "see for yourself." The evidence discovered by forensic pathologists during an autopsy often reveals the exact details of how a murder victim was killed.

Convicting a killer

If someone dies under suspicious circumstances, these are the things that the prosecution has to prove to get a conviction:

- *Who* died, and who killed him or her
- *What* was used to commit the crime
- *When* the victim died
- *Where* the murder took place
- *Why* the murder took place—in other words, the motive for the crime.

Time of death

In the world of films, the time of death is easy to figure out. The pathologist has a quick look at the body, and soon—sometimes even before the autopsy—figures out almost exactly when the person died. In reality, estimating the time of death is far more difficult, and once a person has been dead for more than 48 hours, it becomes harder still. Forensic evidence is usually combined with the evidence of witnesses and circumstantial (background) evidence to produce the closest estimate of the time of death.

"It is frequently helpful to be able to make some on-the-scene judgments as to approximate time of death. Unfortunately, there is no accurate way to establish time of death merely by observing the body. It is far more useful to establish it by other means, such as witnesses, neighbors, unopened mail, or other physical evidence."
Dennis Moyle, law enforcement consultant

Body changes

There are a number of changes that take place in the body after death that can be helpful in estimating exactly when someone died. For example, the normal human body temperature is 98.6°F. As soon as someone dies, that person's body temperature starts to fall, so the temperature of a body will give some indication of how long the person has been dead. However, a number of different things will affect how quickly the body temperature drops. A body will cool down more slowly inside a warm house than if it is on a cold, windy hillside, so the external temperature and weather conditions have to be taken into consideration. A naked body will cool much faster than a clothed body, and a body wrapped in blankets will cool down even more slowly. All of these different factors have to be taken into consideration when using temperature as a guide to the time of death.

Rigor mortis sets in

When a person dies, her or his heart stops pumping blood around the body, and the brain dies within minutes. However, some tissues, like the muscle cells, effectively stay alive for some time after death. When they finally die, the muscle fibers no longer slide smoothly past each other. Instead, they lock solid. This produces a stiffening effect, which is known as rigor mortis. On average, it starts about two to four hours after death and takes between six and eight hours to take full effect.

Other indicators

Other changes that take place in a body at the time of death can be used to help forensic pathologists establish when someone died. Once the heart stops beating, gravity slowly drains the blood to the lowest parts of the body. The top regions become very pale, while the lower regions are dark red. These color changes—known as lividity, livor mortis, or hypostasis—usually begin within a couple of hours of death and become permanent in three to five days. Once lividity is fixed, it can tell us if a body has been moved. For example, if a body is found face downward, but the lividity is visible on the back, it is likely that the body has been moved, perhaps in an attempt to hide it.

Finally, the body begins to decay. Forensic experts use the state of a body to help estimate the time of death. Most bodies follow a similar pattern as they decay. Within two to three days of death, a greenish color begins to appear in some areas of the body, which begins to smell. The body becomes completely discolored, bloated with gas,

Why does rigor mortis differ so much?

The main factor that will decide how quickly rigor mortis sets in is the adenosine triphosphate (ATP) stored in the muscles when the person died. The level of this energy-providing chemical varies from person to person depending on their genetics and their levels of fitness. It also depends on the level of activity before death. For example, rigor mortis usually sets in very quickly in drowning victims, because they have used up all their muscle ATP struggling to stay afloat.

The temperature of the person when he or she dies and the temperature of the surroundings also affect how quickly rigor mortis sets in. But rigor mortis isn't permanent. It usually passes about 36 hours after death, although it can last much longer.

and smells awful. As with all other changes after death, the rate at which these changes take place varies depending on the conditions the body is exposed to.

"The darkest science gives us the understanding and power to help others in the most direct way possible."
Ed Friedlander, pathologist, on introducing forensic pathology to his medical students

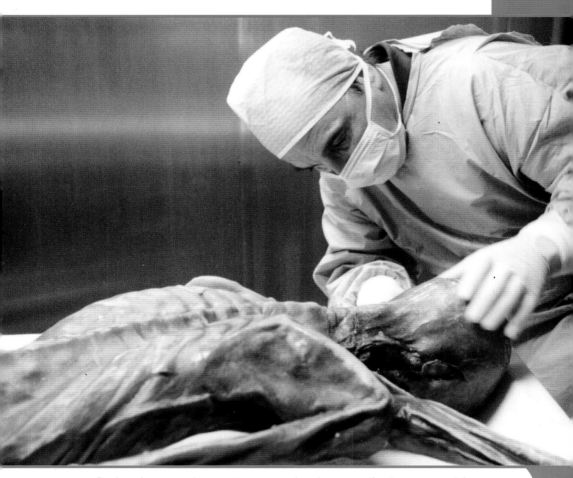

Bodies discovered in icy terrain can be almost perfectly preserved for years. This iceman, nicknamed Ôtzi, was found in the Italian Alps over 5,000 years after he died. On the other hand, bodies left in warm, humid conditions can be reduced to bones in just a few weeks.

Body watching

As you have seen, making an accurate estimate of when someone died is very difficult. So, how can forensic experts make their estimates more accurate? At the University of Knoxville in Tennessee, forensic research teams have been observing in great detail what happens when human bodies decay, in a whole range of conditions. The bodies that they use are donated by individuals who want to help further scientific knowledge in this area. In a secluded site known by the local police as the Body Farm, around 30 bodies are under observation at any one time. Some are buried, and some are not. Some are rolled in carpet or stuffed into garbage bags, some are in damp areas, and others are exposed to the full sun. By monitoring the rate of change in these bodies, the research team can gain invaluable information that will help forensic pathologists all over the world.

Insect evidence

In September 1935, the remains of Isabella Ruxton and her maid Mary Jane Rogerson were found in a ravine on a mountain in Scotland. Many of the women's body parts were found to be infested with maggots. The age of these maggots told the forensic team that the remains had been dumped in the ravine between twelve and fourteen days earlier. This supported the rest of the evidence, which all pointed to Dr. Buck Ruxton as the murderer. He was convicted and hanged in the first recorded case where insect evidence was used successfully in a murder investigation in Great Britain.

Maggots like these appear rapidly in a body, and forensic scientists can use them to help solve crimes.

Estimating time of death

The use of insect evidence in murder investigations has grown steadily. Forensic experts now know the detailed life cycle of blowflies and other insects that colonize dead bodies, and how the life cycle varies under different conditions and temperatures. They can use this evidence to help estimate how long a body has been in the place it is found. For example, if a body found outside had no evidence of blowfly activity, this would tell the forensic team that the body had almost certainly not been there for more than 24 hours. Blowflies often find a body within minutes of death.

The blowfly life cycle

Blowflies are common insects all over the world. They lay their eggs in corpses, including human bodies, and when the maggots hatch, they feed on the body and grow until they form a pupa. Eventually, a new adult fly hatches out. The flies lay their eggs in the natural openings of the body, like the eyes, nose, and mouth, but will also lay eggs in knife and gunshot wounds. The time taken for the life cycle to be completed depends on the temperature, so in cold weather, the maggots take longer to grow than in hot weather. In the hot African country of Zimbabwe, an entire elephant can be reduced to a skeleton in just seven days by maggots and other decomposers.

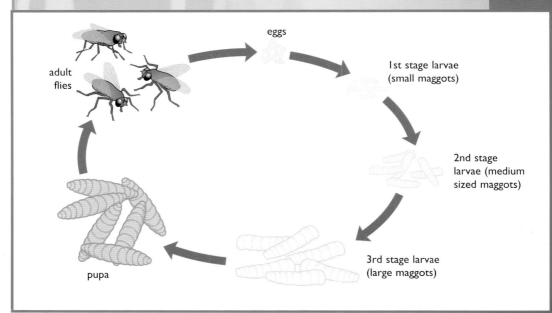

adult flies

eggs

1st stage larvae (small maggots)

2nd stage larvae (medium sized maggots)

3rd stage larvae (large maggots)

pupa

Splatters and Stains

Murders are actually quite rare, and when they do happen, whole bodies are seldom found at crime scenes. However, murderers often leave behind physical evidence—things such as skin, blood, and saliva. These traces are very helpful to the forensic scientist. They can be used to reveal how someone was murdered, who committed a burglary, or who carried out an attack. The technique of DNA fingerprinting, for example, enables forensic experts to identify individuals from small amounts of physical evidence (see the chapter on DNA technology, on pages 44–51).

Scientists collect different materials to help in their investigations. Here, we will look at how one such material, blood, can give valuable information about how and when a murder was committed.

Blood splatters

Violent crime often involves the spilling of blood. Blood is a liquid, so it drips, splatters, and sprays. Blood can be used for DNA testing to identify a victim or a criminal.

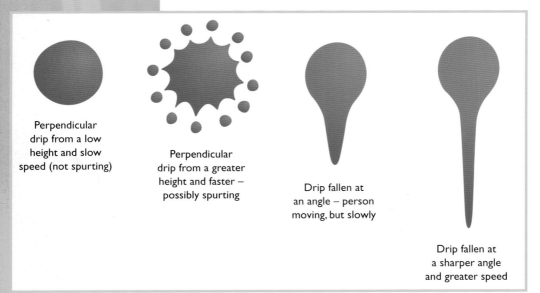

Perpendicular drip from a low height and slow speed (not spurting)

Perpendicular drip from a greater height and faster – possibly spurting

Drip fallen at an angle – person moving, but slowly

Drip fallen at a sharper angle and greater speed

Blood splatters can tell the forensic scientist a great deal about a violent crime. This includes how the victim and the criminal were positioned when the blows were struck and the size of the object used.

The way blood falls can also give important clues about what actually took place. Drops that have dripped from a height have a different shape than droplets that hit a surface at an angle as someone is hit. And as a weapon covered in blood is pulled back from a body, an arc of droplets is produced. The number of arcs of blood tells the forensic scientists how many blows have been struck.

Blood patterns and the lobby killing

In a recent case in Great Briain, forensic pathologist Allen Anscombe was called to a suspected murder in an apartment building. The body was found in a small entrance lobby area between the outer and inner doors, both of which were closed. The floor was smooth and hard. The victim was on the ground and had head injuries. The accused said that there had been a struggle, and the dead man hit his head against the wall or on the bottom of the door. Forensic experts noticed that drops of blood had shot under the inner door, several feet across the floor. This showed them that there must have been substantial impact into the already bloodstained head, such as from a stamp or kick. The victim had been attacked and murdered, and the accused was lying.

"From the nature of the head injuries we thought a fall was unlikely. What the forensic scientists found out about the pattern of blood staining was crucial in establishing he had been murdered."
Dr. Allen Anscombe, a forensic pathologist in Great Britain

Try this!

Try this little experiment, but get permission first! Place a sheet of paper on the floor (it is also best to put lots of newspaper under this sheet of paper, to protect the carpet or flooring that you are working on). Add a few drops of paint or food coloring to some water. Dip your finger into the water and allow a single drop to fall on to the paper from just an inch or two above the ground. Now allow two more drops to fall on the paper, each time from a greater height. The pattern made by the drops will change as the height increases.

Now put drops onto another sheet of paper and tilt it at different angles, watching the different patterns made by the liquid.

Observations on splatter patterns like these help forensic scientists figure out exactly what has happened at a crime scene.

Toxicology and Drugs

One of the biggest problems in the fight against crime in the 21st century is the use and abuse of drugs, both legal and illegal. While the suppliers of illegal drugs are big-time criminals, the local crime that affects most ordinary people is often committed either by people who use drugs (in order to raise the money they need to buy them), or by people who are under the influence of illegal substances or alcohol.

Forensic toxicology involves identifying drugs and poisons in a person's body. It also involves figuring out what effects they would have had.

The breathalyzer allows police officers to carry out an instant analysis of the breath of a suspect. It will show immediately if the person is over the legal alcohol limit for driving a car. Blood or urine samples can be taken later for more detailed analysis.

Blood, urine, and hair

If the police suspect that someone involved in an accident or a crime is under the influence of a drug that may have affected his or her behavior, they will request toxicology tests to see if any drugs can be identified. The drug most commonly connected with crime is actually a legal one: alcohol. But it is not legal to drive a car with more than a certain level of alcohol in your blood, or to attack someone or commit any other crime because the alcohol in your system has affected your behavior. One of the most commonly used and widely known forensic tests is the breathalyzer, which is often used at the scene of traffic accidents.

The three tissues that are most commonly tested for drug abuse are urine, blood, and hair. When a drug is taken, it passes into the blood stream, so for several hours after use it can be measured there. As the body breaks down the drug, other substances are produced. These, as well as the drug itself, can often be detected in the urine for several days. Traces of drugs also build up in hair, where they can be detected for several months. By analysis of body tissues, forensic scientists can therefore not only show that a person has just taken a drug, they can also show that they have been using a drug for some time.

Accuracy matters

Accuracy of testing matters, but even with the most accurate tests in the world, human error can cause problems. In one case, a young man involved in a car accident suffered serious injuries that would affect his ability to work for the rest of his life. His insurance company refused to pay him any compensation (money to make up for the loss) because blood tests done when he was admitted to hospital showed he had opiate drugs in his body. The young man claimed never to have used drugs in his life. When more accurate tests were done on his samples, and the medical staff was interviewed, it turned out he had been given morphine in the ambulance to help with the severe pain he was in. (Morphine is an opiate drug.) When forensic analysis showed that the opiate drug in his blood was medical-grade morphine, the insurance company paid up!

The most accurate way of testing body samples for the presence of drugs is to use gas chromatography to separate the components and then a mass spectrometer to analyze them (see next page).

Gas chromatography and mass spectrometry

In gas chromatography, the substance being analyzed is heated until it vaporizes (becomes a gas). Then the vaporized mixture is carried along a narrow, coiled tube. The different chemicals in the mixture travel at different rates, depending on the weight and size of the molecules within them, so they can be measured at the end of the tube. They are then analyzed further using a mass spectrometer, which fires electrons at the chemicals, breaking them into pieces. The size and relative amount of each piece forms a unique pattern (spectrum), which can be used to identify the chemical. These techniques can be used not only to identify individual drugs, but also to find out how much of a drug is present in the body fluid. The evidence is so accurate that it is accepted in a court of law.

Catching a poisoner

Gas chromatography with mass spectrometry is used to analyze the urine of athletes to check for the use of illegal, performance-enhancing drugs. It is also used to investigate suspicious deaths, drunk drivers, and suspected criminals who may be under the influence of drugs. But the tools of forensic toxicology are not only used in the fight against drug abuse and crime. They can also help catch one of the most secretive types of criminal—the poisoner. Forensic analysis can reveal the presence of poisons in the blood of victims months or even years after death.

Harold Shipman, a doctor dealing death

In 1998, a British doctor named Harold Shipman was arrested for the murder of one of his patients, 81-year-old Kathleen Grundy. In the following year he was also accused of murdering fourteen more of his patients. Police suspect that he probably killed several hundred people. A surprising number of Dr. Shipman's patients died at home after his visits, and some even died in his office. But because they had just seen the doctor, a post mortem was not thought necessary.

Every time someone dies, two doctors have to sign the death certificate. Eventually, a local undertaker and a doctor, who had signed far more death certificates for Dr. Shipman than usual, became suspicious. When challenged, Shipman showed medical notes that explained any unexpected deaths that took place.

Dr. Harold Shipman ran his own practice in the small town of Hyde in Yorkshire. He was well known for his care of his elderly patients, often visiting them at home even when they weren't ill. For all too many of them, Dr. Shipman's visit ended in death. In 2004 Harold Shipman killed himself while serving a life sentence for murder.

Although Kathleen Grundy was 81 years old, she was remarkably healthy and active. Her sudden death, shortly after a visit from Dr. Shipman, which he said was "to take a blood sample for research," came as a complete shock. Relatives found a suspicious will, in which she left all her belongings to Dr. Shipman. But the will failed to mention a second house that Kathleen owned (see pages 32–33 on the forensic skill of detecting forgery, and for more information on this case). Five weeks after she was buried, her body was exhumed (dug up) and body samples were sent for forensic analysis. The tests showed that she had died from a massive overdose of diamorphine, which the court later found had been given to her by Dr. Shipman.

Trace Evidence

Large, solid pieces of evidence, like a bloodstained weapon covered in fingerprints, are obviously of enormous help to a forensic investigating team. However, in most cases, things are not as simple. Fortunately, very small pieces of evidence—such as carpet fibers, strands of hair, flakes of paint, and tiny shards of glass—can be very important, too. Investigators must thoroughly search a crime or accident scene to find these tiny traces of evidence. And it takes the expertise of a forensics department to unlock their secrets. Luckily, recent developments in technology have made the task of investigating trace evidence a little easier.

Under the microscope

Trace evidence is often very small, so the amount of detail you can see with the naked eye is limited. Fortunately, there are many specialized tools to help forensic experts deal with this problem. High on the list are microscopes. The ordinary light microscope reveals many details of small objects. For example, a human hair and an animal hair can look very similar to the naked eye, but the structure revealed by the light microscope can immediately separate you from your dog!

In a light microscope, a beam of light passes through the specimen and then through at least two magnifying lenses to produce an image magnified up to 1,500 times. There are many varieties of light microscopes that can be used to help pick up clues that are completely invisible to the naked eye. For instance, fluorescent microscopy, where the specimens are treated with fluorescent compounds, allow forensic experts to identify specific chemicals or cells.

This is a human hair under a light microscope. A forensic scientist can tell if the hair is natural or if it has been colored or permed.

The images from scanning electron micrographs often look amazing. Who would imagine that the cut end of a pair of tights could look like this? What's more, they can reveal evidence that can convict someone who might otherwise get away with a serious crime.

Super microscopes

Some evidence is too small to be seen clearly even under a light microscope. Then forensic experts turn to an electron microscope. This kind of microscope passes a beam of electrons through the sample to produce an image on a television or computer screen. The level of magnification is enormous—up to 500,000 times! Electron microscopes and the more recent scanning electron microscope, which produces a three-dimensional image, make it possible to see tiny scratches and tears in materials so they can be matched against evidence found elsewhere. It is also possible to identify individual fibers from carpets, ropes, and clothing.

The magnifying power of modern microscopes and the wide availability of the technology have made it possible to use trace evidence in a way that was not possible 30 years ago. And as the technology has moved forward, crime scene investigators have had to develop their powers of observation to collect the tiny pieces of evidence that can now be identified and used. In the past, a torn piece of material was important. Now, it may be a single thread.

Painting a picture

"Paint is a common form of evidence presented to forensic scientists. It can provide valuable evidence that associates a suspect with a crime scene. It might be found on a crowbar, a window, or door; on a hit-and-run victim's clothing; on vehicles in a traffic accident; or as flakes on clothing from a break-in entry point.'

Dr. Allison Jones, forensic expert

Because so many surfaces around you are painted, it may come as no surprise that paint is often involved in a forensic investigation. If paint can be identified, it can be valuable evidence.

The problem with paint is that much of it is very similar. There are millions of walls painted white or off-white, so how can forensic scientists tell that the paint under the fingernails of a victim (or a criminal) came from the house where a crime was committed?

Here again the microscope comes into its own. A single layer of paint gives relatively little information, although it can be used to identify a make and type of car. But often several layers of paint have been applied. This can be seen clearly under the microscope, and in many cases, the different colors of the layers of paint can be identified. This is really useful to investigators. The order of different colors on a wall, or the colors of an old car that has been sprayed and resprayed, tend to be quite unique, and this provides solid, reliable evidence.

But microscopes cannot tell the whole story. Special machines, called colorimeters and spectrophotometers, can analyze and reveal the precise details of the colors present in tiny samples of paint. These machines pass light into a sample and analyze either the light that passes through the sample or the light that is reflected from it. As the techniques continue to develop, it has even become possible to identify different black and white paints or transparent varnishes, using ultraviolet light.

Gotcha!

A young boy riding his bike in Toronto, Canada, was hit by a car. The boy suffered severe head injuries, but the driver did not stop, and there were no witnesses. The police took samples of the paint that the car had left on the boy and his bike. These were analyzed by the forensic team, and the case was kept open on their files. Three years later, local police carried out a routine check of scrap yards for vehicles involved in crimes. They took samples from a car that looked as if it had been in a collision. When the paint was analyzed, it matched samples taken from the injured boy. The police traced the car to its old owner, and the paint evidence helped to convict him of the crime.

Modern forensic technology means that even tiny fragments of paint from an old car, or bits of a car that have been scrapped, can be used to track down a dangerous driver or convict a criminal.

Looking at glass

Crime scenes and accident sites are often littered with glass. When cars collide, lights, windshields, mirrors, and windows shatter, covering the ground, and often the passengers, with glass. When a thief breaks into a car or a house, it is often through a broken window. Tiny shards of glass can remain in clothing and on the soles of shoes for a long time, and as these do not decay and are not affected by washing, they can form very useful evidence. The job of the forensic scientist is to show with certainty where a piece of glass associated with an accident or a crime originally came from.

Density and RI

There are many different types of glass, so forensic scientists use different techniques to show exactly what type of glass a particular fragment is. Sometimes they figure out the density of the fragment, but the most common method of analysis is to use a microscope to calculate the refractive index (RI) of the glass. The sample is placed in silicon oil under a microscope, which steadily gets hotter and hotter. As the temperature increases, the RI of the oil changes until the glass seems to disappear. At that point, the oil and the glass have the same RI, which tells the forensic scientist the RI of the glass itself.

The RI of a sample of glass found at a crime scene can then be used to compare with other glass samples. However, just because two pieces of glass are the same type does not mean that they necessarily come from the same place. That important evidence comes from fracture matching.

Glass breaks in very distinctive ways, and forensic scientists can tell by looking at the patterns of cracks, fractures and stresses in a pane of glass exactly how it has been hit or broken, and from which direction it was hit.

Fitting the jigsaw together

If you tear a piece of paper, you can fit the two pieces together again exactly. Also, if you examine the two torn surfaces under a microscope, you can see the matching patterns on both sides of the tear. This simple fact is the basis of fracture matching, a relatively low-tech forensic skill which has resulted in numerous convictions. If a fragment of torn paper, fabric, or broken glass found on an individual can be linked to a matching fragment found at the scene of an accident or crime, that individual is firmly linked to the incident.

In one case, a body was found that had been cut up and dumped in a garbage can in several black garbage bags, the kind that you tear off a roll. Using fracture matches, forensic teams matched all the bags so that they could figure out the order in which the body parts had been disposed. Then all they needed was the box of garbage bags to match the final bag used for the body parts with the next bag on the roll. Amazingly, when they searched the home of the main suspect, they found a box of garbage bags still under the sink. Sure enough, there was a perfect fracture match for the final body bag, and a murderer was caught.

Although garbage bag rolls like this are perforated to make them easier to tear, each tear is still slightly different to any other. This means fracture matches can be done for each of the bags.

Paper, Ink, and Forgery

Forgery, fraud, and computer crimes may not make headlines as often as murder, assault, and burglary, but these crimes cost millions of dollars each year and often ruin lives. Advances in forensic science are making it easier all the time for the police to identify forgeries and track down the people who have carried them out.

Paper and ink

Money has probably been forged, or counterfeited, more often than anything else in the history of crime. As a result, modern paper money is designed with all sorts of special features to make it as difficult as possible to copy. For example, U.S. dollar bills have a picture of a president and other very small details that are hard to reproduce. The U.S. Treasury Department is always working on making new bills harder to copy, with designs that have more colors in the background or a watermark (a faint image printed into the paper itself).

However, there are many other documents that can also be copied. Checks, wills, passports, ransom notes, and lottery tickets are among the most frequently forged documents.

Records of the different chemicals found in paper and inks have been kept for years, so when the paper and ink of a suspected forgery have been analyzed, they can be compared to the original materials used to see if they are genuine.

For centuries people have tried to forge money to get rich overnight, and for centuries the authorities have done everything they can to make forgery as difficult as possible!

These diaries, supposedly written by Adolf Hitler himself, made millions of dollars for their authors. They must have thought they had gotten away with it, until forensic analysis of ink and paper revealed the clever forgery!

Infrared lighting to show invisible changes, spectrometry to analyze materials, and digital enhancement of samples to see the pattern of the paper fibers are also used to show if something has been added to or removed from an original document.

Case study: the Hitler diaries

In 1981 the editor of Stern magazine in Germany paid $2 million for Adolf Hitler's personal diaries. The diaries were brought to him by Gerd Heidemann, one of his journalists. Two experts compared them to other examples of Hitler's writing and declared them to be real. But some people were suspicious, and in May 1983 the West German police decided to use forensic science to check out the diaries. Forensic analysis showed that the diary paper contained blankophor, a whitening agent that wasn't used until after 1954, when Hitler was long dead. What is more, chromatography showed that none of the four different types of ink used in the diary were available during Hitler's lifetime. And strands of polyester and viscose found in the seals of the documents were not around then either. The documents were clear forgeries, made by a man who specialized in forging Nazi documents. Both the forger and Gerd Heidemann, who set up the plot, were sent to prison.

Print out the evidence

Paper and ink are not the only things that can give away forgeries and reveal fraud. When typewriters have been used to type a note, these notes easily can be traced back to the author, because each typewriter has a unique way of printing the letters. Although computers have largely overtaken typewriters, similar techniques can be used to pin down the printer that was used to produce a piece of written material, and so the ability to analyze typescript forensically still plays a major role in solving crimes.

Computers are increasingly used in crimes such as forgery and fraud. Documents like passports, work permits, and driver's licenses that look real enough to fool most people can all be produced on a computer. To keep up with this new area of crime, computer forensic experts must be aware of all the latest computer technology and how to trace its use. Computer printers can be traced using clues like the level of ink in the cartridge and tiny misalignments in the printer. In addition, the FBI has a huge database of information on typewriters, inks, toners, paper, and watermarks, which forensic experts can use to help them identify the source of forged material. Most important of all, every time someone uses a computer, that person leaves a record. Even when you delete a file, a forensic expert can find a way into the hard drive to uncover a record of what you have been doing.

Forgery and fraud trap a murderer

In the case of Dr. Harold Shipman, who murdered hundreds of his patients (see pages 22–23), forensic scientists investigating a forged will and medical notes on a computer helped uncover a mass murder.

When Kathleen Grundy died suddenly, her daughter Angela Woodruff was completely stunned. She was even more shocked when a lawyer contacted her about her mother's will. Angela was a lawyer herself, and she had always dealt with her mother's legal affairs. The new will was badly typed, and the signature was not like her mother's usual one. The new will left all Kathleen's possessions to Dr. Shipman, but failed to mention a second house that Kathleen owned. It did not take forensic experts long to show that the will had been typed on Shipman's own typewriter, and that the signatures on it were forged. This evidence provided the only clear motive for his crimes.

Hard-drive evidence

Computer forensic experts also investigated the hard drive of Dr. Shipman's computer. It showed that he had frequently changed the medical notes of his patients after they died. He added extra information suggesting that heart disease was developing, which provided an explanation for the patient's sudden death. The way in which Shipman falsified these records weighed heavily against him at his trial in 1999 because it proved that he had planned the murder far ahead. He never admitted any crime, but the forensic evidence of forgery and fraud played a major part in ensuring that he was found guilty and sentenced to life imprisonment. However, he only served four years of his sentence before killing himself in jail.

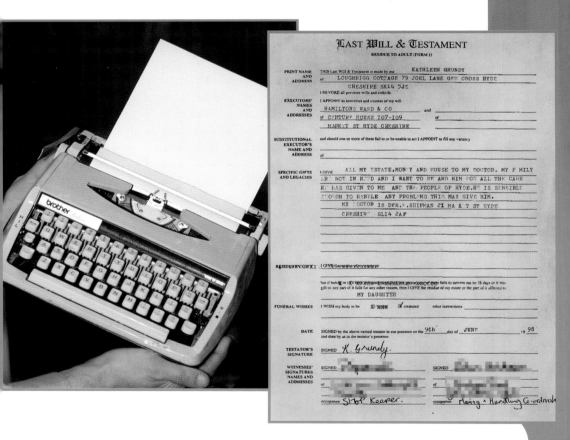

This is a police photograph of the typewriter used by mass murderer Dr. Harold Shipman to type the forged will (right) of his patient, Kathleen Grundy.

Arson, Explosives, and Ballistics

Fire can spread rapidly, burning everything in its path and causing widespread damage and destruction. Most are accidental, but some fires are started on purpose. In the United States, arson costs society billions of dollars each year.

Arson is one of the easiest crimes to commit, but it is also one of the most difficult crimes to detect, as most of the evidence goes up in flames. Fire investigation teams have to make the best possible use of forensic science to help them decide whether a fire has been started on purpose.

Despite the devastating destruction of a serious fire, enough forensic evidence can usually be gathered to show whether the fire was caused by arson or not.

Analyzing the ashes

Forensic investigators take samples of material from the area around the source of fire, including soil from beneath the house, in carefully sealed metal containers to the forensic laboratory. Chemicals contained in the samples are then extracted by distillation, solvent extraction, or headspace extraction so they can be analyzed. The most widely used technique for analysis is gas chromatography (see pages 22–23) although ultraviolet, infrared, and nuclear magnetic resonance spectroscopy as well as flame ionization detectors are also used to identify chemicals. These complex machines not only identify the substances often used to start fires, but also any of the residues that are left behind after a fire has burned out.

Accident or arson?

After a fire, with everything burned and water or foam from fire extinguishers everywhere, it is extremely difficult to piece together exactly what happened. The first thing to identify is where the fire started. This can be done by looking at clues such as the fire marks left on walls. The next question is how the fire started. When arson is the cause of a fire, it almost always involves accelerants—chemicals such as gas, paraffin (wax), and diesel that burn rapidly and with great heat.

A common mistake made by people who commit arson is to think that the evidence of their crime will be destroyed in the blaze. A lot of it is, but the sophisticated methods that have been developed in recent years mean that forensic experts can now pick up traces of accelerants long after a fire has been put out.

"Some time ago I received an e-mail from a 34-year-old American law student called Terri Strickland who had been charged with the murder of her four-year-old son after a fire at her home. She was on bail awaiting trial and she asked me if I could help her… She believed that the fire was accidental and that the fire investigator was wrong in his claim that it was arson. I offered to help her because I know from experience that there is a greater chance of a fire investigator getting it wrong than there is for a woman to murder her child by fire!"

Tony Café, Australian fire investigator (As a result of Tony's work, Terri was found innocent and freed from jail to continue her law studies.)

Explosives

The use of explosives in crime is not widespread, but it can often be deadly. Explosives can be used to gain entrance to vaults or safes when large sums of money or expensive jewels are at stake. But more dangerous is when explosives are used by terrorists. Terrorists use chemicals to make bombs that they may plant in public places, strap to cars to explode when someone gets in, or even strap to the body of a suicide bomber. Forensic scientists have an important role to play in identifying the people who plan and carry out these horrific crimes. Yet because there is such pressure to find the criminals, it is extremely important that the forensic tests available are accurate and reliable. If not, innocent people may end up in prison while the real criminals walk free.

When explosives are used against people, the results can be horrible. Eighteen people died in this suicide bomb attack on a bus in Jerusalem.

When evidence falls short

One way it is possible to identify people who have been involved with explosives is to find traces of explosive materials such as nitroglycerine on their skin, on their clothes, or in their homes. There have been a number of tests available for these substances over the years, including the Griess test and thin layer chromatography (TLC).

Often this evidence is very useful in helping police track down attackers. But without careful interpretation and investigation, this evidence is not enough to prevent future attacks. On February 26, 1993, a van carrying a large bomb drove into the parking garage beneath the World Trade Center in New York. When it exploded, it ripped a hole the size of a football field into the garage. The blast killed six people and injured 1,000 others.

Using forensic evidence from the blast site, the police traced the attack to a group of terrorists living in nearby New Jersey. Two years later, they tracked down and captured the mastermind of the bombing plot, Ramzi Yousef, in Pakistan. The police captured Yousef's computer and found evidence on it that several terrorists were training at flight schools in the United States. Despite this important evidence, the FBI was not able to find these attackers and prevent the second attack on the World Trade Center on September 11, 2001.

Similarly, sometimes evidence leads investigators to make wrong conclusions. This provides that, as much as advances in forensic technology can help solve crimes, it still depends on humans to interpret the evidence correctly and to use it to prevent future crimes.

The significance of the first attack on the World Trade Center "was not fully understood by the critical mass of the United States until September 11, 2001. . . . We just never as a nation responded the way, in my view, we should have responded."
James Kallstrom, former FBI assistant director

Bullets and ballistics

Some of the most upsetting crimes are the ones involving guns. The killer and the victim may have no contact and may not even know each other, and yet one of them loses his or her life. Forensic science plays a large part in solving gun crimes.

Bullet matching

When a gun is made, the barrel is rifled, meaning that it is given spiral grooves that make the bullet spin as it leaves the gun. This makes it travel straighter. As the bullet passes through the gun at high speed, it is scratched and marked by the rifling. Each firearm has its own unique pattern from being rifled, so the scratch marks on each bullet are like a fingerprint from the gun that fired it.

If investigators find a gun that may have been used in a crime, they fire a bullet from it under test conditions. Then they compare the bullet under a microscope to a bullet retrieved from the scene of the crime or from a body. If the marks on the bullets are the same, then the gun was involved in the crime.

Gunshot residues

The gunpowder in bullets usually contains traces of the elements barium, lead, and antimony. If someone is arrested for a gun crime, that person's hands will usually be swabbed and the swabs analyzed using atomic absorption spectrometry. If telltale traces of barium, lead, or antimony are found, it is usually a good indication that the person has recently fired a gun.

Using the relatively new technique of micellar electrokinetic capillary electrophoresis (MECE), forensic scientists can even match a sample of gunpowder to a particular gun. This technique compares the residue found around a gunshot wound with the gunpowder left in a suspect gun. The samples are placed in tiny glass tubes and an electric current is passed through them. The different chemicals move along the tubes at different rates, separating out so that the exact ingredients can be compared.

Entry and exit wounds

When a bullet strikes a human body, it hits with a large force, and as a result, has the potential to cause a great deal of damage. If the bullet goes right through the body, there is often a noticeable difference between the entry and the exit holes.

The entry hole is usually small and smooth, but the exit wound tends to be much bigger and more jagged. The bullet itself becomes squashed and misshapen as it passes through the body. If it gets stuck against bones, it may not exit the body at all. Careful examination by forensic pathologists can reveal the angle at which a bullet entered the body.

If an expert does not examine the victim of a shooting as soon as possible, important evidence can be destroyed. When President John F. Kennedy was shot in 1963, mistakes were made in the confusion following the assassination. For example, one of the bullet wounds was completely destroyed when it was used as the starting point for an emergency tracheotomy (procedure to repair a damaged wind pipe). Because some of the forensic evidence was destroyed in the confusion, people could not agree on the events that day, and many came up with different theories to explain what happened.

It is unlikely that anyone will ever know exactly what happened when President John F. Kennedy was assassinated in 1963. The forensic evidence from the bullet holes in his body was confusing and did not tell a clear story about how he was killed.

Accident Reconstruction

Many accidents involving vehicles happen with no witnesses, and the people involved either are hurt and unable to talk about the incident or just find it hard to remember what happened in the confusion of a crash. Fortunately, there are specialized teams that can reconstruct accidents using forensic evidence collected from the site, showing exactly what has happened. This is partly to find out if someone committed a crime, such as by driving dangerously or under the influence of alcohol.

At the scene

A lot of the work of accident reconstruction is carried out at the scene of the accident. The police and the accident reconstruction teams take photographs that clearly show the positions of the vehicles involved, skid marks on the road surfaces, and weather conditions at the time of the accident.

Skid marks like these on the road can help police and forensic experts reconstruct exactly what happened when an accident took place.

Analyzing skids

Skid marks can help police estimate the minimum speed the car was traveling when it started to brake. They can indicate if a driver was traveling too fast for the road conditions at the time of the accident. Analyzing skid marks is a skill that requires a good understanding of math and physics. There are around 22 different mathematical formulas that can be used to help figure out exactly what a set of skid marks means. One of the simplest, and most commonly used, is the basic speed skid formula:

$$S = \frac{V^2}{30f}$$

where S is the length of the skid, f is the coefficient of friction (for a normal tire on a dry road, f is about one) and V is the velocity (speed) of the car when it started skidding, which is what the investigators want to know.

For example, if a skid is 82 feet long, $82 = \frac{V^2}{30 \times 1}$

so $\quad 82 \times 30 = V^2 \quad$ so $V = \sqrt{2{,}460} \quad V = 90$ feet/sec

So the speed of the car when it started to skid was around 62 miles an hour.

Headlights on or off?

All too often in an accident, one person will claim to have been doing one thing, while other witnesses say exactly the opposite. For example, one person might claim to have had his or her regular headlights on, while another might claim that the person had on his or her brights. Fortunately, forensic scientists are often able to figure out who is right. In the case of headlights, the glass is almost always shattered in an accident. The metal filaments of the light bulbs are exposed to the oxygen in the air, and an oxidation reaction takes place. The hotter the metal, the more oxidation there is. When headlights are on bright or high beam, the metal filaments in the bulb are hotter than when the lights are on low beam. By measuring how much oxide there is on the filaments, scientists can tell whether headlights were off, on bright, or low beam at the moment of impact.

Disaster

Trains, boats, and airplanes can also be involved in crashes. Although the number of deaths and injuries in traffic accidents each year is greater than the number in any other type of disaster, train, boats, and planes tend to make the news when they crash because they involve so many people at the same time.

When a large passenger plane crashes, the enormous force of the impact spreads debris over a very wide area, often several square miles. After such an accident, forensic teams and accident

The 1998 Lockerbie plane crash was devastating—259 people lost their lives on the plane and 11 lost their lives on the ground. Accident reconstruction experts and forensic scientists work for months and even years after a disaster like this to piece together the wreckage and find out exactly why the plane crashed.

reconstruction experts try to collect every piece of debris that can be found and use it to help reconstruct exactly what happened. They examine pieces of metal under the microscope to look for signs of metal fatigue, or evidence of an explosion. Experts also rebuild the aircraft from its pieces to try to find out how and why the disaster took place. In addition, they analyze information from the in-flight recorder—called the black box—using special computers to enhance the sounds heard. When all the evidence has finally been gathered, it is usually possible to figure out what went wrong.

The Lockerbie disaster

On the evening of December 21, 1988, Pan American Flight 103 was on its way to New York after a stop at London's Heathrow Airport. At 31,000 feet, as the plane flew over Lockerbie in Scotland, a bomb blew apart the plane. All 259 passengers and crew on the plane died, and 11 people were killed on the ground by falling debris. Wreckage and body parts were strewn over an area of many square miles. The forensic science and accident reconstruction teams pieced together information to show that Flight 103 been the target of a terrorist bomb.

Michael Charles, the chief air accident investigator in the Lockerbie bombing, went to court to describe the horrible effects of the explosion. Using models and diagrams and referring to evidence of many different types, Charles showed exactly where and how the damage to the aircraft had occurred. A bomb in a suitcase had been planted in the left front cargo area. If it had exploded just a few minutes later, the wreckage and bodies would have fallen into the Atlantic Ocean. There would have been no reconstruction, no evidence, and no trial. Instead, as a result of the work of the investigative teams, the relatives of the victims know exactly what happened to their loved ones. And because it was shown to be a terrorist attack, the people who carried out the crime could be identified, tracked down, and brought to trial.

DNA Technology

Who you are, from your hair color to your shoe size, depends on your DNA. DNA is the genetic material that carries the blueprint of life. Found in the nucleus of the cells of your body, it contains information inherited from both of your parents. Everything from your physical appearance to your personality depends, at least in part, on your DNA. DNA is a very long molecule in the shape of a helix, or spiral. It is made up of only four different subunits, which are joined together in many different combinations.

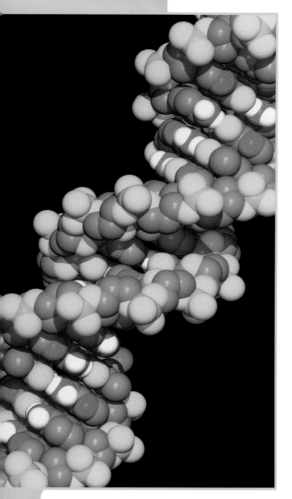

DNA, the helix-shaped molecule, can be used to identify criminals.

Unless you have an identical twin, your DNA is unique. Other members of your family will have strong similarities in their DNA, but each individual has her or his own unique blueprint. Only identical twins have the same DNA, because they both develop from the same original cell.

What does all this information have to do with forensic science and solving crimes? The biggest single development in forensic science in the last hundred years has been the ability of forensic scientists to identify individuals from the DNA left behind in traces at the scene of a crime. Bodily fluids, such as blood and saliva, as well as fragments of skin can provide the DNA needed to identify a criminal or to prove that someone is innocent.

DNA fingerprinting

In 1984, Dr. Alec Jeffreys and his team at Leicester University in Great Britain were the first people to develop what we now call DNA fingerprinting. They were looking at the DNA that makes up your chromosomes.

How does DNA fingerprinting work?

In DNA fingerprinting, the strands of DNA from a sample are chopped up into fragments using special enzymes known as restriction endonucleases, which cut the DNA at particular points. The fragments are placed on gel plates containing dyes that react to DNA, and then separated using electrophoresis. The smaller DNA fragments move farther than the larger ones. The finished plate has dyed bands of DNA, and the darker the color of the band, the more DNA fragments of that type there are. This technique results in what is known as a DNA fingerprint, which is unique to the individual. DNA found at a crime scene can be compared with the DNA of a suspect. A match gives the investigating team strong evidence of guilt.

Large chunks of DNA do not actually carry any useful information. These regions of your chromosomes are often called junk DNA. Dr. Jeffreys' team discovered that these junk areas produce clear patterns when they are chopped up and stained to make them visible—patterns that are very different in each person. However, Dr. Jeffreys also noticed that they were more similar between people who were related than between total strangers. The team realized that this might be a good way to identify criminals or to prove innocence. It is extremely unlikely that two identical samples would come from different people (apart from identical twins), so the technique proved very useful for forensic scientists.

DNA fingerprints like these can be used to prove guilt or innocence in a crime investigation.

Convicted

DNA fingerprinting has had an amazing impact on the ability of the police both to identify criminals and to prove that people are innocent of crimes. The first ever murder conviction that was brought about as a result of DNA evidence was in Great Britain. The same technology also cleared a man of rape and murder in the same case.

In 1983, fifteen-year-old Lynda Mann was murdered in Narborough, in Great Britain. Evidence showed that she had also been raped. A semen sample was taken from her body, but at that point scientists could tell the blood type and little else from the evidence. Three years later another fifteen-year-old girl, Dawn Ashworth, was found murdered in the same way, in the same area. All the evidence pointed to it being the work of the same man. The semen samples showed that the blood types matched.

The police had a suspect, a local man who eventually confessed to Dawn's murder but denied having anything to do with Lynda's death. The police officers in charge of the case, Chief Constable Michael Hirst and Chief Superintendent David Baker, were convinced that if he had committed one crime, he must have committed both. They contacted Dr. Alec Jeffreys, who had published work showing how new DNA analysis techniques—what is now called DNA fingerprinting—could be used to help solve crimes. When Dr. Jeffreys ran a comparison between the semen collected from the bodies of both the victims and the blood of the suspect, he found that the same man had certainly carried out the crimes. But it was not the man who had confessed!

Superintendent Baker then decided to set up a mass screening of all the adult males in the three towns in the area where the girls had lived and died. Samples were gathered from 5,000 men, and DNA profiling was carried out on the men who had the same blood type as the murderer. But nobody's DNA matched that of the killer. What else could be done?

An overheard word cracks the case

Even with the DNA evidence, the killer might have gotten away with it and killed again if it had not been for an overheard conversation. A local woman heard someone boasting that he had given his DNA sample in a false name. He had done a friend a favor and claimed to be Colin Pitchfork when he gave his saliva sample. The woman went to the police, the real Colin Pitchfork was arrested, and DNA samples were taken. Sure enough, when the results came back, Pitchfork's DNA profile matched that of the semen taken from the murdered girls. The police, with the help of some very new biotechnology, had caught the killer. In 1988 Colin Pitchfork was jailed for life for the two murders.

In the days before DNA fingerprinting, Colin Pitchfork would almost certainly have gotten away with his crimes and been free to murder again.

The polymerase chain reaction

When DNA fingerprinting was first developed, large samples of material were needed to carry out the analysis. Although the new technique was amazingly successful and made a huge difference to crime investigations, the amount of DNA needed really limited how often the new technique could be used. However, another amazing scientific development soon came along to solve the problem. The polymerase chain reaction (PCR) has changed both molecular biology and DNA technology. It made it possible to produce large quantities of DNA from very small samples in a remarkably short time, and the DNA produced is all identical to the original. This means that tiny samples of DNA left at the scene of a crime can be analyzed. Even the tiny amount of saliva left on the rim of a water bottle is enough to help convict a criminal!

Every time a cell in the body makes a copy of itself, the DNA in the nucleus is copied. The DNA molecule unzips, and the enzyme DNA polymerase makes a copy of the separated strands. Using the DNA polymerase enzymes from a bacterium that lives in hot springs in Yellowstone National Park, a scientist named Kary B. Mullis developed a technique for copying DNA artificially in the lab. His idea worked, and he won a Nobel Prize in 1993 for developing PCR.

Kary B. Mullis discovered the polymerase chain reaction. The process has enabled forensic experts to identify criminals from tiny traces of DNA.

How does PCR work?

In the polymerase chain reaction, lots of copies of a single strand of DNA are made very quickly. The enzymes used from the bacterium *Thermus aquaticus* control the different stages of the copying process at different temperatures. A tiny sample of DNA is mixed with all the ingredients for making more DNA, plus the special enzymes. The temperature of the mixture is then changed at regular short intervals, and the tiny sample can be copied again and again to produce millions of identical DNA molecules—enough to carry out DNA fingerprinting.

The development of PCR means that scientists can now analyze minute DNA traces left at crime scenes today. But it also means they can go back to crimes committed many years ago and use modern technology to track down the offenders.

Since the development of PCR and its use by police forces around the world, some people who must have thought they had gotten away with a crime are now being brought to justice. Police forces are looking back over old, unsolved cases and bringing out evidence such as bloodstains in the hope that these cases can be solved. DNA has proved to be a tough molecule that survives for years. With PCR, even the smallest traces of DNA can be copied to provide enough for scientists to produce a DNA fingerprint. This is the technique that helped convict the murderer of Helena Greenwood (see pages 4–5).

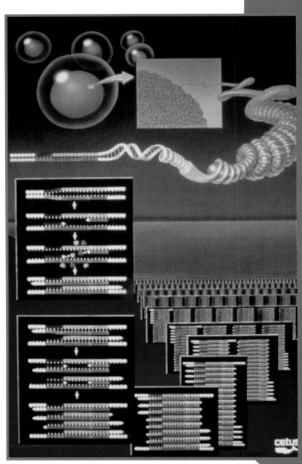

This diagram shows the polymerase chain reaction. The two strands of the DNA are split apart (top box), and the two primers (blue and green) are added. The area to be copied (orange and yellow) is filled in by supplying the chemical building blocks of DNA with the enzyme DNA polymerase. Repeating the process produces millions of identical copies (lower right).

DNA analysis—yes or no?

Despite its usefulness, DNA evidence is not completely reliable. DNA profiles usually use only part of our DNA. Most of the time this level of DNA fingerprinting is accurate enough to identify a person correctly, but things can go wrong. A man named Raymond Easton from Pinehurst, Great Britain, suffers from Parkinson's disease. By the year 2000 he was so disabled that he could hardly dress himself without help. In spite of this, he was charged with a burglary that had taken place 200 miles away from his home! The error arose because four years earlier, Raymond had been involved in a family argument that gotten out of hand. The police had cautioned him and taken a sample of his DNA. By an amazing coincidence, Raymond's DNA matched that found at the scene of the burglary.

Once a more thorough DNA analysis was made, differences between Raymond's DNA and that of the burglar became clear, and the charges against him were dropped. In this case, DNA analysis solved the problem it had caused.

National DNA database

The development of PCR and the use of the copied DNA to produce unique DNA fingerprints have brought many exciting developments in crime detection.

The FBI operates a nationwide database known as CODIS, which stands for the Combined DNA Indexing System. Containing DNA samples from prison inmates across the country, CODIS has helped local police and investigators track down suspects in more than 11,000 criminal cases. It has also helped free prisoners who were wrongly convicted of crimes they did not commit.

Today CODIS contains DNA samples from more than 1.6 million criminals. Each month local police officers gather between 10,000 and 40,000 new samples and add those to the database. Thanks to CODIS, thousands of cases have been solved, including a number of cases that went unsolved for years.

Privacy concerns

With the success of CODIS, some people are pushing for a nationwide database that contains samples of DNA from everyone in the country. Some people are happy to support a database like this, as it certainly would help police identify criminals and make convictions. However, there are some people who are worried about the impact of DNA technology on society. These people are concerned about the rights of individuals not to have their identity on a police system.

Supporters claim that there would be many important benefits from a national database. They would include improvements in health care, an increased ability to find the guilty person in any crime committed, and a country where it is much harder for terrorists to take on false identities.

On the negative side, people fear that their DNA might be used against them by the police. There is also the concern that the information would be made available to insurance companies that might refuse insurance or demand huge premiums (monthly payments) based on DNA information showing a tendency to develop certain diseases. And false matches, as in the case of Raymond Easton, might become more common.

The debate over using DNA in this way continues, but one thing is certain—DNA fingerprinting is here to stay, and many more criminals will be brought to justice as a result.

The tiny traces of saliva on a water bottle or drink can provide enough DNA to identify someone.

Computers and Crime

Computer technology has had a huge impact on crime detection over the past 30 years. With their ability to store huge amounts of data, recognize patterns, and work at incredible speeds, computers have helped scientists and police officers use information in a completely new way. Investigating teams no longer depend on local evidence and local knowledge alone. Now they can tap into national and even international resources to help them identify and convict a criminal.

Computer technology increasingly means that police forces in different parts of the world can share information about criminals or missing people.

National Crime Information Center

In 1967 the FBI developed a computerized system that would completely change the way local police officers tracked down criminals. Known as NCIC, which stands for the National Crime Information Center, the system was able to store thousands of police records, which state and local police could access from anywhere.

Today the system contains millions of records with information on criminals, missing and unidentified persons, violent gangs, and terrorists. Since it began, it has helped solve thousands of cases, including helping police track down Oklahoma City bomber Timothy McVeigh. Police officers and sheriffs across the United States—and even outside the country—now have access to millions of records at the touch of a button.

Psychological software

Scientists are constantly coming up with new ways of using computers in the fight against crime. A team of forensic psychologists (scientists who study the mind) recently developed a software program that links psychological profiles of the way different burglars work with the patterns of burglaries in an area. Detailed forensic evidence collected from every crime scene is fed into the computer. As a result, the police can not only pick out likely suspects, but also predict which areas are most at risk. This, in turn, helps the police prevent crime and pick up criminals by being on the spot as the crime is committed.

Identifying faces

Computers have also changed forensic work. Eletronic images, based on evidence provided by witnesses, can help identify criminals, missing persons, and murder victims. The big advantage of computers is that they allow an almost unlimited number of slight variations to be made to the picture of a face. And witnesses can see these pictures right away. What is more, forensic pathologists can use them to help reconstruct the possible appearance of murder victims when bodies are found after a long period of decay. When people have been missing for a long time, computers can be used to age their faces to show how they may look now.

Criminals on the run can be shown with and without facial hair or with their hair dyed and cut differently to help people recognize them and report them to the police.

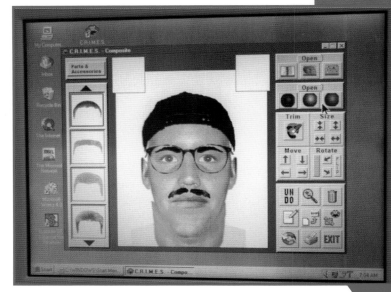

As computer technology develops, forensic scientists and pathologists can provide information about an unidentified body or reconstruct the face of a murdered person.

Computers and car crime

There are millions of cars on the roads, and thousands of these vehicles will be involved in crimes of some sort. Increasingly, there is a network of cameras positioned on main roads, constantly filming the flow of traffic beneath. The images are so clear that the license plates of the vehicles can be identified, and in some cases, the people in the cars are visible as well. All of the information collected is fed into computers that record the position and speed of the vehicles. It can then be used to fine drivers who are driving too fast or dangerously, and to track criminals in stolen vehicles and identify their position so police patrol cars catch them.

Developments in both camera and computer technology mean that evidence from traffic cameras can reveal where you were at a particular time of day, and what you were doing!

None of your business!

In many parts of the world, cameras are becoming more and more common in public places. Closed-captioned television cameras, known as CCTV cameras, can be found in many major cities, such as London, England. They are designed to catch shoplifters and prevent vandalism and muggings. However, when more serious crimes take place, the footage often provides useful evidence. When the London train bombings took place in July 2005, pictures from CCTV cameras across the city showed the identities of the bombers. After that, many people in the United States said they thought CCTV cameras should be used in American cities as well. But others spoke out against this technology, arguing that it would be an invasion of privacy. Today the discussion continues, and people are still trying to figure out the best way to balance safety with privacy.

Reconstructing events

Forensic investigations into road traffic accidents usually provide lots of evidence that accident investigators can use to figure out exactly what has happened. The same is true for train crashes, boating accidents, and plane crashes. New developments in computer technology have made it possible to reconstruct events using computer animation. All the information known about an accident can be fed into a computer, and it can show what would happen if vehicles behaved in the way suggested. These reconstructions are now allowed in the courts. They have been used both to confirm accounts of an accident and also to show clearly that a defendant could not possibly have been driving in the way they are claiming.

Computers across national boundaries

Computers have changed the face of forensics, allowing information to be processed in seconds and matches to be made almost instantaneously. Information about investigations and the results of forensic testing can be shared with people in other countries at the click of a mouse. As computer technology advances, and police forces across the world establish more international databases, criminals are going to find it harder and harder to escape the penalties of the law.

The Future of Forensics

In the 21st century, new technology will allow forensic science to move out of the lab and onto the crime scene itself. Already, an image of a fingerprint taken at the scene of a crime sometimes can be identified immediately through an on-site computer link. In the future, using satellite link-ups, it may be possible to check such evidence at the scene against an international line-up of suspects!

In addition, the DNA databases that various countries are building are likely to expand to cover almost everyone on the planet. This might mean that, in the future, forensic experts will be able to identify a criminal on the spot, at the scene of the crime. For some time to come, forensic analysis will depend on people as well as technology. But it is a serious concern for forensic experts that much of the work that used to depend on human expertise is being taken over by ever more intelligent machines.

Moving on

Forensic scientists are pushing the boundaries of science all over the world. Some of the work involves dealing with computers and other sophisticated machines. Other work involves examining decaying bodies and developing faster ways of establishing the evidence of crimes. For example, when someone is murdered, it often takes a long time to find the body, and this makes it harder to catch the murderer.

Arpad Vass, forensic researcher at the Body Farm at the University of Tennessee, is attempting to build an instrument that will help police locate a body earlier. And with any luck, it will help police figure out exactly when the victim died. His work involves a detailed analysis of all the chemicals produced by a body as it decomposes in the ground, using gas chromatography and a mass spectrometer. Vass aims to identify particular chemical compounds produced through the decomposition process and develop a hand-held instrument that can be used like an electronic sniffer dog to pick up tiny traces of the compounds.

What will the future hold?

With all the developments in technology in the past 30 years, the science of forensics seems limitless. And as newer technologies and techniques become available, detection and conviction will become even easier and more reliable. Every contact leaves a trace. In the future, crime scene investigators may be able to link those traces straight to the person who made them, using machines connected to powerful computers that will immediately carry out the analysis. This would effectively end the need for detectives and forensic experts. But will it put an end to all crime, and therefore the need for forensic science? Some say so, while others believe that human error and corruption will never go away. What will the future of forensic science hold? There is no clear answer, but what is clear is that the years to come will bring many exciting—and probably controversial—developments in forensic science.

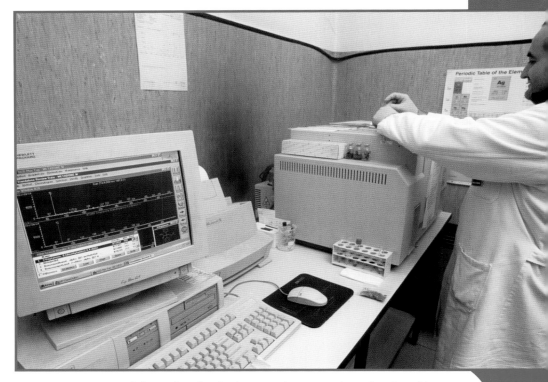

A forensic scientist is preparing a sample to be placed in a mass spectrometer. The display screen on the left will show the sample's chemical composition and allow small traces of both known and unknown material to be detected.

Timeline

700 The Chinese use fingerprints to identify the owners of documents and clay sculptures, although there was no formal classification system of prints.

1784 John Toms is found guilty of murder in Lancaster, Great Britain, because a torn piece of newspaper on the murder weapon is found to match another piece discovered in his pocket. This is the first time physical matching is used to secure a conviction.

1835 Henry Goddard, an early police officer, uses bullet comparisons for the first time to catch a murderer.

1880 Henry Faulds presents his idea that unique fingerprints at a crime scene might be used to solve the crime.

1892 Sir Francis Galton publishes the book *Fingerprints*, largely based on the work of Henry Faulds.

Argentina becomes the first country to officially adopt the use of fingerprints to identify criminals after Juan Vucetich shows how effective it can be.

1900 Karl Landsteiner discovers human blood types. Max Richter adapts the technique for forensic use to identify the blood type of bloodstains associated with crimes.

1901 Sir Edward Henry at Scotland Yard in Great Britain pioneers the regular use of fingerprints to identify criminals. In the United States, Henry P. DeForrest does the same thing.

1908 The Federal Bureau of Investigation (FBI) is formed in the United States.

1910 Edmond Locard in France establishes the first modern police crime lab.

1925 Saburo Sirai, a Japanese scientist, shows that some people secrete blood-type-specific antigens into other body fluids, and this can be used to help identify or eliminate suspects.

1935	The Buck Ruxton case is the first use of insect evidence to convict a murderer.
1940	Vincent Hnizda is the first chemist to analyze ignitable fuel (used in arson attacks) using vacuum distillation.
1954	The breathalyzer test for identifying the alcohol levels in the breath is developed and brought into use.
1960	Gas chromatography is used for the first time in forensic investigations.
1977	Fuseo Matsumur and Masato Soba figure out a method of making latent (hidden) fingerprints appear using the fumes from superglue.
	The FBI introduces the Automatic Fingerprint Identification system.
1984	Dr. Alec Jeffreys develops DNA fingerprinting at Leicester University in Great Britain.
1985	Kary B. Mullis publishes his work on the polymerase chain reaction, which he discovered in 1983. It enabled the tiniest samples of DNA to be reproduced to provide a large enough sample for DNA fingerprinting.
1986	Colin Pitchfork becomes the first person convicted of murder on DNA evidence.
1991	A Canadian company launches an automated imaging system for comparing the marks on bullets and guns.
1999	Helena Greenwood's murderer is brought to justice as DNA technology is used to solve old cases.
2000	Parkinson's sufferer Raymond Easton is accused of a burglary on the basis of DNA tests, but more detailed testing revealed his innocence.
	Dr. Harold Shipman is convicted of murder as a result of a combination of forensic techniques.
2003	Scientists discover the complete sequence of the human genome, opening the way to even more accurate identification of people in the future.
2004	Harold Shipman commits suicide in jail, carrying with him the truth about exactly how many murders he committed.

Glossary

adenosine triphosphate (ATP) molecule that supplies the energy needed for a wide range of metabolic (energy-burning) processes, such as the mechanical work performed by muscles

arson setting fire to property or land on purpose

atomic absorption spectrometry passing light through materials to produce a pattern of lines representing the colors absorbed by different types of atoms

autopsy medical examination of a dead body

bacterium (plural **bacteria**) microorganism that can be beneficial or cause disease

biochemist scientist who studies the chemistry of living organisms

breathalyzer device used to measure chemicals (usually the alcohol content) in the air you breathe out

CCTV camera closed circuit television camera often used for security purposes in cities and inside stores

cell basic unit of all living organisms

chromosome structure made of DNA found in all living cells. It contains the genetic information that is passed from one generation to the next.

coefficient of friction measure of how easy it is for one surface to slide over another

convict/conviction decide that someone is guilty of a crime in a court of law

density measure of the compactness of a substance

deoxyribonucleic acid (DNA) substance found in the nucleus of a cell that carries the genetic code

distillation method of separating a substance from a solvent or two or more solutions from each other using evaporation and condensation

DNA fingerprinting technique that analyzes the patterns in the junk DNA that are unique to each individual

DNA polymerase enzyme that helps copy a tiny DNA sample in the polymerase chain reaction

electron sub-atomic particle with a negative charge that surrounds the nucleus of an atom

electron microscope microscope that uses a beam of electrons to see tiny objects that are too small to be seen clearly using a light microscope

electrophoresis special form of chromatography in which substances are separated by an electric field rather than by a moving gas or liquid phase

enzyme biological catalyst that speeds up or controls chemical reactions in the body

evidence information used to prove or disprove a fact in court

exhumed when a corpse that has already been buried is dug up

fluorescent something that absorbs energy from ultraviolet rays and re-emits it as visible light

forensic evidence scientific information used to solve crimes

forensic toxicology identification of drugs and poisons in the solution of a crime

Griess test chemical test to reveal nitrite residues that uses a number of different chemicals

iodine chemical element

mass spectrometer instrument that ionizes atoms and molecules and uses electric or magnetic fields to measure the mass/charge ratio of the ions produced. It can be used to accurately identify chemicals.

minutiae point small variation on the basic fingerprint pattern that is unique to each person

nuclear magnetic resonance spectroscopy way of analyzing substances based on the way the nuclei of the atoms behave in a strong magnetic field

opiate drug drug made from opium (the dried juice of a poppy plant)

oxidation chemical reaction in which an atom or ion loses electrons

polyester synthetic polymer used to make plastics and clothing fibers

polymerase chain reaction (PCR) series of reactions that produce large quantities of identical DNA from a very small original sample

post mortem an examination of the body after death. In the case of suspicious deaths, this is carried out by a coroner.

rape unlawful sexual intercourse without a person's consent

refractive index (RI) measure of how a material bends light

rigor mortis stiffening of the muscles after death

scanning electron microscope microscope that moves a beam of electrons across the surface of a specimen to create a highly magnified three-dimensional image

solvent extraction method of extracting substances depending on the solvent in which they will dissolve

spectrometer instrument that measures the wavelength of electromagnetic radiation, including visible light

terrorist person who carries out criminal acts directed against a country that are intended to create fear in the minds of particular people or the general public

thin layer chromatography (TLC) method of separating substances where a thin layer of solid phase, called alumina, is applied to a glass plate

toxicology study of poisons and toxins and their effects on the body

tracheotomy opening made into the trachea (wind pipe) through the neck so that a tube can be put in place to make breathing possible

viscose synthetic polymer used, among other things, to make clothing

Further Reading

Books

Fullick, Ann. *Science Topics: The Human Body*. Chicago: Heinemann
Library, 1998.

Dowswell, Paul, Paul Mason, and Alex Woolf. *Forensic Files* series.
Chicago: Heinemann Library, 2004.

Websites

**http://pbskids.org/dragonflytv/parentsteachers/tguide_forensics
.html**
This website, sponsored by PBS, contains lots of easy-to-read
information about forensics as well as games and riddles.

http://www.pbs.org/wgbh/nova/archive/int_fore.html
This website has links to famous cases involving forensic science.

http://www.nationalgeographic.com/features/97/andes
This National Geographic website contains information about an
autopsy performed on an Inca girl found perserved in Peru.

Index